Funky Fiends

Edited By Andy Porter

First published in Great Britain in 2023 by:

Young Writers
Remus House
Coltsfoot Drive
Peterborough
PE2 9BF
Telephone: 01733 890066
Website: www.youngwriters.co.uk

All Rights Reserved
Book Design by Ashley Janson
© Copyright Contributors 2023
Softback ISBN 978-1-80459-777-4

Printed and bound in the UK by BookPrintingUK
Website: www.bookprintinguk.com
YB0557E

Foreword

Young Writers was created in 1991 with the express purpose of promoting and encouraging creative writing. Each competition we create is tailored to the relevant age group, giving each child the inspiration and incentive to create their own piece of writing, whether it's a poem or a short story. We truly believe that seeing it in print gives pupils a sense of achievement and pride in their work and themselves.

Our latest competition, Monster Poetry, focuses on uncovering the different techniques used in poetry and encouraging pupils to explore new ways to write a poem. Using a mix of imagination, expression and poetic styles, this anthology is an impressive snapshot of the inventive, original and skilful writing of young people today. These poems showcase the creativity and talent of these budding new writers as they learn the skills of writing, and we hope you are as entertained by them as we are.

Contents

Ackworth School, Ackworth

Vivi Gledhill (11)	1
Vida Adler (10)	2
Gabriella Bowerman (11)	4
Darcie Nazeri (10)	6
Scarlett Hall (8)	7
Heloise Schoukroun (11)	8
Imogen Johnson (11)	9
Oscar Scoukroun (11)	10
Henry Bradley (10)	11
Grace Reilly (8)	12
Rose Thornton (11)	13
Cameron Welke (8)	14
Bethan Hill (11)	15
Annie Foster (7)	16
Sofia Livock (11)	17
Jacob Line (11)	18
Milana Meakin (11)	19
Mia Flynn Burton (8)	20
James O'Brien (8)	21
Stefan Azamfirei (11)	22
Josh Macdonald (8)	23
Frank Hunter (8)	24

Ardersier Primary School, Inverness

Maisie Taylor (8)	25
Ella-Mai Christison (9)	26
Destiny Sutherland (10)	27
Elsie Shanks (9)	28
Beau Rooney (9)	29
Piper Watson (8)	30
Rudi Ising (8)	31
William Robin (9)	32

Bridekirk Dovenby Primary School, Cockermouth

Harriet Dodds (8)	33
Olivia Bell (8)	34
Georgiana Moore (8)	36

Cyfarthfa Park Primary School, Cyfarthfa Park

Noah Healey (9)	37
Daria Mioduszewska (8)	38
Catrin Burns (9)	40
Pearl Brogden (9)	42
Hattie Lewis (9)	44
Ryan Willoughby (8)	46
Harper-Rose Slocombe (8)	48
Elizabeth Morgan (9)	50
Gwen Williams (9)	52
Bobby-John Holt (9)	54
Thomas Cross (9)	55
Hudson Medlicott (9)	56
Isabelle Jones (9)	57
Danny Hyder (9)	58
Millie Cook (8)	59
Millie Price (8)	60
Celyn Needs (9)	61
Harri Luckwell (9)	62
Amelia-Jayne Sibley (9)	63
Olivia Joneso (9)	64
Isaac Johnson (8)	65
Layla Snare (9)	66
Jamie Treharne (8)	67
Ralph Cooper (9)	68
Hope Menzies (8)	69
Ellie Hegarty (9)	70

Evelyn-Rose Abbas (8)	71
Alexander Bailey (8)	72
Riley Butler (9)	73
Cameron Martin (9)	74
Scarlett Pocknell (9)	75
Jacob Roman Lewis (9)	76
Sophia Gunter (9)	77
Alys Hocking (8)	78
Kainan O'Rourke (8)	79

Gulval School, Penzance

Rio Richardson (10)	80
Beau Nash (10)	83
Jonty	84
Amy Nudd (9)	85
Riley Marment (10)	86
Dexter Cudmore (9)	87
Freya Mann (10)	88
Oliver Harvey (10)	89
Liliana Uddin (10)	90
Mya-Rose Thomas (10)	91
Jason Stacha (10)	92

Hasland Junior School, Hasland

Molly Barnett (8)	93
Georgia Price (7)	94

Immanuel And St Andrew CE Primary School, London

Victoria Lupak (8)	95
Cecily Chandler (7)	96
Ada Vening (7)	97
Noah Gilson Organe (8)	98
Keya Edmonds (8)	99
Cesia Ester Medina (7)	100
Jagoda Lakos (8)	101
Leila-Marie Stewart (8)	102
Matiya Kouakou (8) & Mariette Kouakou (8)	103
Maya Barczyk (8)	104
Grace Wikeley (8)	105

Jack Leevi Dean (8)	106
Zuzanna Szmulska (8)	107

John Rankin Junior School, Newbury

Lily Johnson (9)	108
Anushka Joshi (9)	109
Isobel Healy (9)	110
Phoebe Avarne (9)	111
Emily Allan (9)	112
Nilesh Sharma (9)	113

Miller Academy Primary School, Thurso

Emily Budge (9)	114
Skye Brock (9)	115
Georgia Donogher (8)	116
Charlie Valente (9)	117
Maisy Campbell (9)	118
Lana Simpson (8)	119
Charlie Litchfield (9)	120
Adam Clark (9)	121
Fraser Mill (8)	122
Seth Pollard (9)	123
Darcey Shearer (9)	124
Struan Sparling (8)	125
Anya Livingstone (9)	126

Revoe Learning Academy, Blackpool

Nevaeh King (9)	127
Layth Essaadi (8)	128
Cayla Sowerby (8)	129
Holly Sharman (9)	130
Xander Wood (9)	131
Ramy Essaadi (8)	132

St Mary's RC Primary School, Edinburgh

Ryan Conlisk (8)	133
Coburn Dalli (8)	134
Amelie Prestage (8)	137
Agnes Johnston (8)	138

Strabane Primary School, Strabane

Emma Patterson (9)	140
Cameron Foy (9)	141
Farrah Mcgerrigle (9)	142
Max Thompson (9)	144
Alex Hamilton (9)	145
Paige Porter (9)	146
Aoibhi Brolly (9)	147
Emma Devine (9)	148
Aaron Kingham (9)	149
Blaine Peoples (9)	150
Emily McCully (9)	151

The Poems

Spirit And The Coronation

Spirit sat alone in his cave,
With no coronation flag to wave.
Everyone was partying in the streets,
Whilst Spirit had no friends to meet.
It's because I'm a monster! he thought,
Maybe I just ought -
"What are you doing here all alone?"
Said a monster with green fur,
What's she doing? Spirit thought,
What is wrong with her?
"I'm here to take you to a party,
No one deserves to be alone!"
So, for the first time, Spirit had lots of fun
And left his home.
From then on, Spirit gained lots of friends,
Because when you start to meet people,
The fun never ends.

Vivi Gledhill (11)
Ackworth School, Ackworth

What Will He Do?

In the depth of the night,
Far up on a hill,
Lived a frightening monster,
Was it ready to kill?
Inside his cave,
He slurped on what could be someone's poodle.
But was it? No!
It was just some spaghetti noodles!

Nuhowii put on his cloak,
His gloves and his shoes.
Everyone in town wondered,
What would he do?
Nuhowii stomped into town,
His feet going *thump, thump!*
The villagers also heard
The *bump, bump, bump.*

A little girl, fast asleep,
Was sleeping on the ground.
He turned his head
And looked around.

After that, Nuhowii yawned,
For he was tired too.
The girl awoke and screamed,
"What will he do?"

Nuhowii tried to reassure her,
But she was far too frightened.
So even after funny faces,
Her mood was not lightened.
Nuhowii began to cry
And pulled up his hood.
This monster was the definition
Of misunderstood.
As he stalked back to his cave,

Nuhowii cried, "What will I do?"

Vida Adler (10)
Ackworth School, Ackworth

There Is A Monster In My Head

There is a monster in my head
And I just can't get him out,
When I try to concentrate
He starts to scream and shout.

There is a monster in my head
And he says things that he shouldn't,
But if I tried to get on
He'd say we really couldn't.

There is a monster in my head
But in exams he is very useful,
When I ask him the answer
He is always very truthful.

There is a monster in my head
And he is really, really cute,
But he is super-duper noisy
In his hefty red boots!

There is a monster in my head
And he has purple spots,
But his dinky little horns
Are covered in green dots.

There is a monster in my head
And he has little wings,
He flies around my mind
Whilst he beautifully sings.

There is a monster in my head
And I don't want to get him out,
If you try to take him
I will give you a great big pout!

Gabriella Bowerman (11)
Ackworth School, Ackworth

Friendly Fudge Looks Ferocious

Fudge and Scrabble love to play all day
They don't understand why other yetis run away.
The yetis don't like Fudge because he is so unique
It's such a shame the outlook's so bleak.
Scrabble cares so deeply about his scary-looking friend
They'll be best friends forever until the very end.
An odd new yeti finds herself an outcast from the pack
But Fudge and Scrabble are so kind they would never send her back.
Fudge, Scrabble and Rio became the most magnificent trio
And never spent another day caring about what the other yetis had to say.

Darcie Nazeri (10)
Ackworth School, Ackworth

Dude The First

Let me introduce you to my monster called Dude,
He is always in the most cheery mood,
He loves to sing, dance and play,
But things don't always go his way.

He's not just a monster, he's a shape-shifter, you see,
He likes to try to shape-shift into a tree,
But poor old Dude made a mistake,
Instead of a tree, he turned into a snake!

Dude was at the coronation of our king and queen,
He was so excited he tried not to scream,
He tried to shape-shift into Queen Camila's gown,
But instead, he became King Charles III's crown!

Scarlett Hall (8)
Ackworth School, Ackworth

Cannot!

The monster cannot help being scared.
The cactus cannot help being prickly.
The cave cannot help being dark and gloomy.
And I cannot help being furry.

Even in my sleep, I dream of how unlucky I am.
Even in my sadness, I love my fun.
It keeps me nice and warm, even in the coldest of times.

I swim in the rivers of my tears.
I climb through the mountains of my grief.
I travel for years and years.
And on the other side Furry, beautiful Furry.
His gloomy cave, shining in the moonlight.

Heloise Schoukroun (11)
Ackworth School, Ackworth

Zigabung Goes For A Friendly Stroll

Once upon a time in sunny San Diego's streets
A friendly blue monster I think you'd like to meet
Zigabung skipped and hopped, exploring every place
Greeting people with a smile on its friendly face
In the heart of the city, its laughter echoed loud
Bringing joy and happiness to the beaming crowds
Zigabung had a talent for listening and caring
Understanding each person, their joys and their sharing
With a heart full of kindness, it lent a helping hand
Making San Diego's streets a wonderland.

Imogen Johnson (11)
Ackworth School, Ackworth

A Goopy Little Smile

A goopy little smile, that's what Cuddles has,
When he cheers you up, it's like smooth jazz.
As he clings to you with all his might,
You'll be as calm as a koala, without a fright.
Eating all his sweets, and gumballs,
Do not give him soda or he'll be bouncing off walls.
Cuddles likes to travel all over the place,
Putting a smile on everyone's face.
A goopy little smile, that's what Cuddles has,
When he cheers you up, it's like smooth jazz.

Oscar Scoukroun (11)
Ackworth School, Ackworth

Da Thing

Da Thing only creeps out at night,
It's not looking for a fight,
But its next meal for its tum,
It likes the crunch of humans, yum!
It drags its victim to its cave,
It doesn't take time to rant or rave.
It gobbles them up in one bite,
However, its tummy is finite.
After it has had its fill,
It takes an anti-constipation pill.
If he forgets he doesn't have to wait,
To end up in such a state,
That it explodes.

Henry Bradley (10)
Ackworth School, Ackworth

Cutie The Beauty

I met a monster on my street,
She was purple with curly feet.
Her name was Cutie, she was a beauty,
She wanted to play, I said, "That's okay.
We can go to the park,
Until it gets dark."
Going home,
I met a gnome.
He said, "Hey, how is your day?
I want to play."
I said, "We're flesh and bone,
But you're made of stone."
So we danced around the gnome,
Then we went home.

Grace Reilly (8)
Ackworth School, Ackworth

Friend Or Foe?

Nelly came from Sweden,
To find her freedom,
To paint or draw,
That was for sure.

She flew over here,
Nattering into the ear,
Of any creature that could hear her,
Be it covered in feathers or fur, it could hear her.

Nelly was very kindhearted,
So she got the party started,
Splashing paint all over her friends,
And dishing out magical pens.

Friend or foe,
Nelly will be kind to you!

Rose Thornton (11)
Ackworth School, Ackworth

Worry William

My monster William is like a rainbow
I see him from my bedroom window
I know he'll always be my buddy.

Outside in his den, he has a mailbox
Which he empties every day
When he lights it up he always drops
A lot of worries to wish away.

I used to be scared of the worry monster
Until he saw me worrying
He waved and said, "What are you worrying about?"
And I said, "Nothing."

Cameron Welke (8)
Ackworth School, Ackworth

Linvy

Linvy,
Lovely, generous, benevolent.
She's not mean or dangerous.
In fact, she's full of playfulness,
Everyone always judges her,
As everyone towers over her,
Why she tries to see people smile,
But she only gets a pile of dullness,
Her bow is her best feature,
She is a loving creature,
But there's one thing she loves more than the rest...
Her Grizzalog, of course,
I love Linvy!

Bethan Hill (11)
Ackworth School, Ackworth

Tango The Tarantula

T ango the tarantula, two foot one
A lways scary, never fun
R ichard is Tango's naughty friend
A nd their tricks never end
N aughty mischief, it is always in the house
T hey creep about as quietly as a mouse
U nder the moonlight, they run fast
L urking under rocks, hidden at last
A fter all their scaring they go to sleep.

Annie Foster (7)
Ackworth School, Ackworth

Kasma And I

Kasma and I went for a walk
In a beautiful meadow
Filled with stunning, sunset-coloured roses.
After our stroll, we went snorkeling
In the crystal blue sea of Hawaii.
A while later, Kasma took me to her house,
Which was a colossal, underwater cave
Where the only entertainment
Was watching metallic fish swim,
One after the other.

Sofia Livock (11)
Ackworth School, Ackworth

Is This A Dessert?

On the peaceful journey to school
I spotted a creature which was a gooey green
He wasn't a dessert on the loose
And he was taller than six foot two
His teeth were razor blades
Yet he was a friendly monster too
We played on the swings
And swung on the branches too
It was such a fun day
And he said he would be back soon.

Jacob Line (11)
Ackworth School, Ackworth

The Gentle Giant

A dinosaur once roamed the Earth,
A gentle giant of great worth.
His scales were soft, his heart so true,
A friend to all, old and new.

He roamed the Earth with a happy smile,
And made friends that would last a while.
Together they laughed, they played, they roared,
A group of friends that could never be bored.

Milana Meakin (11)
Ackworth School, Ackworth

The Day I Went To School

On the way to school,
I met a monster, fluffy and funny.
She looked like a cat,
And she licked my hat.
She was a friendly monster from the rainforest,
Purest, cleverest, sincerest.
We played the piano,
She shape-shifted into a flamingo.
Today was a fun day,
We said goodbye and then she flew.

Mia Flynn Burton (8)
Ackworth School, Ackworth

Glider Tim The Monster

Glider Tim, you'll never see him
He hides in a cave
So try to be brave
His skin changes colour
So he can blend in
Hide-and-seek is what he plays
But you'll never win
Glider Tim, the monster I know
He loves his cave and isn't that scary
It just goes to show.

James O'Brien (8)
Ackworth School, Ackworth

Jelly

Jelly is from the Maldives
That's where he still lives
He lives in a hut
On the edge of a wood
He sometimes is invisible
And he can be big trouble
He plays the banjo
And can juggle
And get into a muddle
But in the end
He is very loveable.

Stefan Azamfirei (11)
Ackworth School, Ackworth

Penshar

One Tuesday morning when I woke,
I put on my slippers and felt a poke,
To my surprise, a monster popped out,
It was Penshar playing about,
With his great big shark fin
And his big, bright, yellow feet,
He gave me a big, great sweet.

Josh Macdonald (8)
Ackworth School, Ackworth

Slimy Monster

Once there was a monster.
They were very big and slimy.
And it was very happy and always got hot
And the slime was so hot it would burn your skin.
It was taller than a house
And wider than a ten-metre-long wall.

Frank Hunter (8)
Ackworth School, Ackworth

My Poem (By Daffodil)

I'm cute but I don't have a flute.
I'm furry but my name's not Murray.
I'm a mermaid but I've got no fade on my face.
I don't have love but I'm a dove.
I can shape-shift into anything you want but sometimes I haunt.
I can fight but I'm not alight.
My name's Daffodil because my name's not Will.
I'm a cherry, not a berry.
I can catch but I don't match.
I've got two eyes but I don't compromise.
I'm from London and don't have a button.
I can maybe mend but this is the end.

Maisie Taylor (8)
Ardersier Primary School, Inverness

Molly Is A Kind Monster

Molly is a monster.
Molly has no friends.
Molly gives lollies just to be friends.
Molly meets Holly!
Molly gives a lolly so that they are friends.
Holly takes the lolly, now they are friends.
Molly and Holly see a boy called Olly.
Molly gives a lolly, now they are friends.
Molly sees a bunch of lollies.
Molly takes the lollies.
Olly takes her lollies and says,
"You're way too much of a bully!"

Ella-Mai Christison (9)
Ardersier Primary School, Inverness

The Monster Holly

Holly is a monster.
Holly has friends.
Holly meets Molly.
Holly takes the lolly from Molly
So that they become friends.
Holly and Molly meet a boy called Ollie.
Molly sees a bunch of lollies.
Molly takes the lollies.
Ollie takes the lollies from Molly.
"You're a bully," said Molly.

Destiny Sutherland (10)
Ardersier Primary School, Inverness

The Poem About Bob

Bob is nice but still so scary
And he is rather hairy.
He is from the forest where it's dark
But it's good for when it's rainy
Because he can take a walk to his friend's balcony
And have a disco party.
He likes to stay at his friend's house
And play with his mouse.

Elsie Shanks (9)
Ardersier Primary School, Inverness

Monster Poetry - Funky Fiends

The Werewolf

My werewolf's name is Midnight,
This werewolf has two friends,
They go on full-moon strolls,
And climb up high mountains.

They run at the speed of lightning,
And jump up to the moon,
She can transform when it's dawn,
And howl when it's noon.

Beau Rooney (9)
Ardersier Primary School, Inverness

My Monster

My monster is the best
My monster is an alien in space
My monster really is the best
My monster can be a robot
My monster will be the best
My monster
My monster will be the king
My monster will be the king of Paris.

Piper Watson (8)
Ardersier Primary School, Inverness

Cheesy Chicken Mecha Pasta

Cheesy Chicken Mecha Pasta has some friends
He's the master of the world
But one day he went to a gig
And he ate a fig
Cheesy Chicken Mecha Pasta loves everyone
He is mega
He eats peas and loves people.

Rudi Ising (8)
Ardersier Primary School, Inverness

About Seek

Seek only has a friend named Vision 2.0
They were born on the red planet Mars
He likes Star Wars movies
And he has lightsabers and the Force.

William Robin (9)
Ardersier Primary School, Inverness

Monster Poetry - Funky Fiends

Monsters Are Crazy

When I woke up on a sunny day
A monster popped up and wanted to play
Bubble bubble bubble
A monster is in trouble
When I went downstairs and opened the door
I saw monsters playing more and more
When I looked around on the lawn
I saw a monster called Curly Horns
Bubble bubble bubble
A monster is in trouble
When I came home from school today
All the monsters wanted to play
When I looked around to take a look
They were drawing in a big book
Bubble bubble bubble
A monster is in trouble
The monsters were tired
So they got fired
So they went out of the house
As silently as a mouse.

Harriet Dodds (8)
Bridekirk Dovenby Primary School, Cockermouth

Cookie Monster

Hi, I'm Cookie Monster
How are you?
I love cookies
More than you!
Round ones, flat ones
I like to eat them all
For breakfast, dinner
And tea 'n' all
I like to go shopping
To get a tasty treat
But seem to scare everyone
I see in the street
They scream and they yell
I think, *please do tell*
How can a monster
Be as scary as hell?
They look in horror
As I enter through the bakery door
Some even hide themselves
On the bakery floor!

But in their fright
With the sinister sight
Stands a monster
Who they might actually like
I might be big
I might be loud
But I'm very proud
To be the happiest monster around
I buy my cookies
And take a bite
Before sharing them out
With everybody in sight!

Olivia Bell (8)
Bridekirk Dovenby Primary School, Cockermouth

Alush's Daily Routine

I wake up in the morning,
I always start by yawning,
I start by playing the flute,
But whilst I play my brother puts me on mute,
I get dressed,
I like to look my best,
I go on the zombie bus,
And run to school in a rush,
Music lessons and recorder sessions,
Goodbye school,
Goodnight Youl,
(Goodnight Mum in monster language),
I need a sandwich!

Georgiana Moore (8)
Bridekirk Dovenby Primary School, Cockermouth

The Hungry Monster

The hungry monster always loves bacon
He eats it every night
But he is always woken
By the sun being too bright.

He loves food extremely, coffee and toffee
Early morning he eats it in a hurry.

My monster looks weird
He looks like a can
Everyone drinks him
And he hates fizzy drink bans.

He likes to eat and gobble food down
Tesco is empty and Asda
Because he ransacked town.

The hungry monster always loves bacon
He eats it every night
But is always woken
But the sun being too bright.

Noah Healey (9)
Cyfarthfa Park Primary School, Cyfarthfa Park

My Monster Is A Furball!

My monster loves to play hide-and-seek,
She's actually very fat.
She takes her friend's pug into a lab,
To turn the pug into a hat.
My monster loves to munch on Doritos,
And she also likes to munch on mosquitos.
She eats toffee and she drinks coffee,
But she doesn't like salad.
My monster is as furry as a lion,
Her eyes look like a cat pleading.
My monster's teeth are as small as a baby,
And her ears look like a Floppa's.
My monster likes to play tag,
She also likes to run.
But she doesn't like walking,
Because she feels like a snail walking.
My monster will be a hero,
She will always save the world,
She is the strongest furball in the world.
My monster loves to play hide-and-seek,
She's actually very fat.

Monster Poetry - Funky Fiends

She takes her friend's pug into a lab,
To turn the pug into a hat.

Daria Mioduszewska (8)
Cyfarthfa Park Primary School, Cyfarthfa Park

My Little Monster

My monster from out of space,
She loves to sing and dance,
But if you get close to her,
She'll put you in a trance.

My little monster likes to eat,
She does it all the time,
She always likes to eat coffee and toffee,
I don't know why.

My monster is fluffy,
As soft as a teddy,
She has big blue eyes,
And is always cuddle ready.

My monster likes to sing and dance
She does it all the time
She enjoys it so much
She thinks she's a ballerina in the sky!

My monster went to a Hollywood show,
To show she's a superstar,
And is ready to glow!

Monster Poetry - Funky Fiends

My monster from out of space,
She loves to sing and dance,
But if you get close to her,
She'll put you in a trance.

Catrin Burns (9)
Cyfarthfa Park Primary School, Cyfarthfa Park

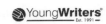

Terrific Trevor

Terrific Trevor
Likes to eat ticks and crunchy fleas
But doesn't have any manners
So won't say please.

I took him to the park
Where he finally said, "Please"
But it was getting dark
And we didn't want to freeze.

He's like a vast old greedy pig
That eats and eats all day long
His favourite food was a sour fig
But now it's onions, which is so wrong!

Trevor always lazes around
Rolling on his back, bottom or belly
He's like a big heap on the ground
Even when he's watching the telly.

Terrific Trevor
Likes to eat ticks and crunchy fleas
But doesn't have any manners
So won't say please.

Pearl Brogden (9)
Cyfarthfa Park Primary School, Cyfarthfa Park

The Monster That Came From Candy Land

My monster likes to eat delights,
He says they are delicious.
If he doesn't get his food in time,
He will turn malicious.

My monster likes sweets,
Even knowing he gets bad teeth.
He doesn't even care,
Brushing his teeth is rare.

My monster is pink,
He has blue eyes.
He has his tongue sticking out,
And very big in size.

My monster likes to fly,
He's barely on the floor,
He flies up so high.

He sees a portal,
So he jumps right in,
Landing with a grin.

My monster likes to eat delights,
He says they are delicious.
If he doesn't get his food in time,
He will turn malicious.

Hattie Lewis (9)
Cyfarthfa Park Primary School, Cyfarthfa Park

The Amazing Monster

My monster has an ugly body,
Sometimes he drinks squash,
He's also pretty shoddy,
And he's always needing a wash.

My monster named Jim,
Loves to eat toffee,
He also has a limb,
My monster also drinks coffee.

Jim the gargantuan monster,
Has great big blue eyes, as big as a star,
He has smooth skin,
He is literally Vimto.

My monster's hobbies are drinking Vimto,
Also playing football,
Another one is rugby,
And his final one is having a short fall.

My monster has an ugly body,
Sometimes he drinks squash,
He's also pretty shoddy,
And he's always needing a wash.

Ryan Willoughby (8)
Cyfarthfa Park Primary School, Cyfarthfa Park

The Monster That Bumps His Head

My monster likes to go to the park.
But often bumps his head.
Because he always plays in the dark,
"I need glasses," he says.

My monster likes to eat raw chicken.
His belly is ten feet.
You often see him eating some meat.
And fills one hundred seats.

My monster is as big as a car.
He also has ten eyes.
And six ears.

My monster likes to go to the park.
And also has lots of fun.
He likes to roll around in the mud.
Especially in the sun.

Monster Poetry - Funky Fiends

My monster likes to go to the park.
But often bumps his head.
Because he always plays in the dark.
"I need glasses," he says.

Harper-Rose Slocombe (8)
Cyfarthfa Park Primary School, Cyfarthfa Park

My Mucky Ducky

My monster is from under my bed
Where he turns very red
He loves to eat fresh human flesh
He says it's really tasty
A bit like pastry.

He is cute and cuddly
His name is Ducky
He is colour changing
Wow, that's amazing!
He loves to get mucky, that's lucky.

I'd be mad but it's not half bad
He loves what he does, making me laugh
When he's breaking the bed in half.

He sleeps like an otter
He is a puppy
Time to say goodnight
Under the moonlight
Till another day
Hooray!

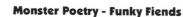 

My monster is from under my bed
Where he turns very red.

Elizabeth Morgan (9)
Cyfarthfa Park Primary School, Cyfarthfa Park

Slime Google

My slime monster
He is as slimy as a baby
When he is hungry
He is as fierce as a bear
So beware.

My monster likes to eat dry fish
He swishes his teeth
It happens very rarely
He doesn't do it very often.

He looks very slimy and gooey
And like Milky Bars.

He likes to eat
And make a beat.

He falls out of bed
And bumps his head
And he says
"Owee, that hurt."

My slime monster
He is as slimy as a baby
When he is hungry
He is as fierce as a bear
So beware.

Gwen Williams (9)
Cyfarthfa Park Primary School, Cyfarthfa Park

My Hairy Monster

As the sun sets he will give you a fright
My monster likes to roll around in leaves
And when he comes out he has leaves in his hair
Some say he looks like a tree
His favourite food is chicken and chips
He always licks it and bites it
The blue, hairy monster is as thin as a single post
My monster likes to eat and sleep, it's his favourite
My monster is rich, he has lots of money
My monster likes to roll around in leaves
And when he comes out he has leaves in his hair
Some say he looks like a tree.

Bobby-John Holt (9)
Cyfarthfa Park Primary School, Cyfarthfa Park

The Monster Who Eats Children

Zog is a monster and can be wild.
His favourite food is a delicious child.
My monster likes to eat a delicious child.
They always smile and have to be wild.
My monster is red and never goes to bed.
He has red eyes.
He has sharp nails.
Zog is not a sporty monster but he likes to hunt children.
He bought a child shredding machine.
My monster always lies but his heart never dies.
For some reason he puts children into pies.
Zog is a monster and can be wild.
His favourite food is a delicious child.

Thomas Cross (9)
Cyfarthfa Park Primary School, Cyfarthfa Park

All About Dreamy

Hi, my name is Dreamy, I come from the planet Creamy
I like to wash my feet to keep them very cleany
I like to eat creamy monster bars
The monsters I eat are very hairy and really like to bark
I am a slimy melted Maoam ball
And a super hairy wolf.
I am a deadly terrifying T-rex
The monsters I eat are so slimy
I am like a dumb baby
So I get taken to jail
It is dark, quiet, not a sound
Hi, my name is Dreamy, I come from the planet Creamy
I like to wash my feet to keep them very cleany.

Hudson Medlicott (9)
Cyfarthfa Park Primary School, Cyfarthfa Park

The Little Hiding Monster

Hi, my name is Reggie, I like to eat veggies,
I live in a forest and I'm very honest.
My favourite food is cupcakes and they are very sweet,
Just like a bowl of ice cream.
I'm rainbow-coloured like a bag of Skittles,
I'm fuzzy and fluffy all over my body.
I like to do art, I think I'm an artist.
People find the forest I live in and I hide away from them,
Because I am sneaky like a spy.
Hi, my name is Reggie, I like to eat veggies,
I live in a forest and I'm very honest.

Isabelle Jones (9)
Cyfarthfa Park Primary School, Cyfarthfa Park

Everything About Fred

The monster is as lazy as a sloth
And he likes to eat human bone broth,
He really likes to eat human flesh
Because it makes him feel very fresh,
My monster is really hairy
If you look at his face he will look very scary,
My monster likes to hide in the coat rack with his various pack
And when he goes he doesn't leave a track,
Fred is too lazy to get off his bottom
He is so short he is like a mini wardrobe,
The monster is as lazy as a sloth
And he likes to eat human bone broth.

Danny Hyder (9)
Cyfarthfa Park Primary School, Cyfarthfa Park

My Monster And I

My monster likes to snuggle with me
But sometimes he would rather drink tea
After that, he will come back to snuggle.

My monster and I, sitting in a tree
My monster and I, drinking some tea
My monster and I, having caffeine.

My monster's favourite food is pizza, pasta
Chocolate, custard
Coffee, toffee
My monster is as skinny as a window.

My monster likes to snuggle with me
Sometimes he would rather drink some tea.

Millie Cook (8)
Cyfarthfa Park Primary School, Cyfarthfa Park

Cool Monster

My monster is ugly,
But he's also very cool.
Watch out, he's very hungry,
And lives in a deep pool.
My monster likes toffee,
But he drinks coffee.
My monster has four arms,
But he has four legs.
My monster likes football,
But he also crawls.
My monster dies badly fast,
But he comes back to life.
My monster is ugly,
But he's also very cool.
Watch out, he's very hungry,
And lives in a deep pool.

Millie Price (8)
Cyfarthfa Park Primary School, Cyfarthfa Park

Monster Poetry - Funky Fiends

The Monster From Mars

There is a colossal, vast monster
He has big, vast, long eyes
He has a master smasher blaster
But sometimes he cries
My monster looks like an alien
And his friends look like him
And he also plays 'The Sims'
He loves to eat food
But sometimes he doesn't like it
But he is in a bad mood
There is a colossal, vast monster
He has big, vast, long eyes
He has a master smasher blaster
And sometimes he cries.

Celyn Needs (9)
Cyfarthfa Park Primary School, Cyfarthfa Park

My Monster Boby

Hi, my name is Boby
I'm big and bad
Don't eat my chocolate
Or I'll get monster mad
I like to eat ice cream and berries
I've got chocolate on my face
I look like a disgrace
Swinging my hate all over the place
I like to eat chocolate
I'm a big and bad monster
I get bigger
Hi, my name is Boby
I'm big and bad
Don't eat my chocolate
Or I'll get monster mad.

Harri Luckwell (9)
Cyfarthfa Park Primary School, Cyfarthfa Park

The Demon Monster

He is a monster
But he is not cute
His eyes are red
Because he is underfed

He likes to eat meat
With a cup of cherries
His legs are like demons
His horns are like bulls

He likes to sleep
Because it makes him smell his stinky feet
He likes to make a mess
Because he is in a dress

He is a monster
But he is not cute
His eyes are red
Because he is underfed.

Amelia-Jayne Sibley (9)
Cyfarthfa Park Primary School, Cyfarthfa Park

My Monster Strawberry

Hi, my name is Strawberry
I am from the planet Fluffy
When I eat chocolate frogs
My face goes puffy.

My eyes are as big and blue as blueberries
My fur is like pink bubblegum
I like to scare
I creep around
I went back to Fluffy
And exploded with cuteness and rainbows.

Hi, my name is Strawberry
I am from the planet Fluffy
When I eat chocolate frogs
My face goes puffy.

Olivia Joneso (9)
Cyfarthfa Park Primary School, Cyfarthfa Park

My Monster

My monster is a greedy pig, he loves to climb
His legs are fast and he does it in record time.
My monster likes eating people
And he likes them so much.
My monster is a big spider
And he is the size of a fridge.
My monster likes to climb in time
And he gets Prime.
He loves them
And drinks them.
My monster is a greedy pig, he loves to climb
His legs are fast and he does it in record time.

Isaac Johnson (8)
Cyfarthfa Park Primary School, Cyfarthfa Park

Blobby The Blob Monster

I am from Jupiter, my name is Blobby
Scratching my bottom is my favourite hobby
I'm slimy, fat and cute
I like to play the flowery flute
I am green and snobby
As slimy as a slug
I have antennae like a butterfly up in the sky
I have a red nose like Rudolph
I'm a greedy pig for ice cream
And I think it's time for *monster school!*
Scratching my bottom is my favourite hobby.

Layla Snare (9)
Cyfarthfa Park Primary School, Cyfarthfa Park

Friendly Monster

Hi, my name is Iggy Boogie
And I live with Boogie Woogie.
I am humongous and fun.
I like to sit in the sun.
My favourite food is pizza
But my favourite flavour is Margherita.
I'm fluffy, cute and rainbow-coloured
Like a multicoloured Skittle.
I like to be coached and like to be kind.
I made friends with everyone.
I'm humongous and fun.
I like to sit in the sun.

Jamie Treharne (8)
Cyfarthfa Park Primary School, Cyfarthfa Park

Sweaty, Gymnastic Ronadol!

My monster is fat
He loves to eat
He is like a rat
And fills up one hundred seats
He is lazy
But crazy
He is a greedy pig
When he eats
And he gigs
He is gigantic but fat
Like a rat
He has custard
With some mustard
Dough balls and bacon
Milkshakes but not shaken
He has eyes like a fish
Like a dish
He comes morning, noon and night.

Ralph Cooper (9)
Cyfarthfa Park Primary School, Cyfarthfa Park

My Monster

My monster is from Mars
My favourite things are chocolate bars.
My monster loves to always eat ice cream
He eats it just like a pig.
My monster is flat and fluffy
He is red and yellow like McDonald's.
My monster loves to go to a play place to hide from me
Especially in the ball pit.
My monster is from Mars
My favourite things are chocolate bars.

Hope Menzies (8)
Cyfarthfa Park Primary School, Cyfarthfa Park

My Monster

My name is Starry
I am cute and hairy
I came from London
Sometimes I am scary.

I like to eat berries that are sweet
Because they are my favourite treat.

I am as cute as a puppy
I am as sweet as cotton candy
I am as fluffy as a cloud.

My name is Starry
I am cute and hairy
I came from London
Sometimes I am scary.

Ellie Hegarty (9)
Cyfarthfa Park Primary School, Cyfarthfa Park

Cucumber The Monster

Hi, my name is Cucumber
And I am from Planet Freezer
And my best friend is called Riot Reever.
He likes to eat pig
With a bit of twig.
Green and mean
But he is like a little machine.
I lie in bed all day
And then snore away.
Hi, my name is Cucumber
And I am from Planet Freezer
And my best friend is called Riot Reever.

Evelyn-Rose Abbas (8)
Cyfarthfa Park Primary School, Cyfarthfa Park

Monster Shape-Shifter

The monster struggles with his emotions
But he wants himself to not struggle

He eats fruit and bugs but not hugs
He has one eye and big wings and stripes

My monster plays in the trees
He falls out of the trees and gets stung

The monster struggles with his emotions
But he wants himself to not struggle.

Alexander Bailey (8)
Cyfarthfa Park Primary School, Cyfarthfa Park

My Monster Larry

My name is Larry.
And I'm in love with Gary.
I like to eat human arms for tea.
I cover them with salt, it makes them taste better.
It's a good treat for me to eat.
I like to hide in the pitch-black dark.
I shape-shifted into a dog and someone took me.
My name is Larry.
And I'm in love with Gary.

Riley Butler (9)
Cyfarthfa Park Primary School, Cyfarthfa Park

My Deep Monster

Bob's favourite job is to kill to get his bill
Bob likes to eat his meat to make him fresh and full
He has two eyes, two horns and a big black chest
Teeth as sharp as Shrek's teeth
His favourite hobby is human-killing
Unfortunately they aren't willing
Bob's favourite job is to kill to get his bills.

Cameron Martin (9)
Cyfarthfa Park Primary School, Cyfarthfa Park

My Monster

Iggy Iggy likes to eat fish and chips after a summer sleep
Iggy Iggy likes to eat ice cream after something sweet
My monster is not cute at all, he is like a pig when he eats socks
My monster's favourite hobby is sleeping like a sloth
Iggy Iggy likes to eat fish and chips after a summer sleep.

Scarlett Pocknell (9)
Cyfarthfa Park Primary School, Cyfarthfa Park

My Monster

Tall, strong and very hairy
Lucifer is truly scary
Crunching bricks
Munching sticks
Adding chicks to the mix
His rough, rocky skin
Is as bulging as fresh lava
He likes to sleep very deeply
He likes to walk and talk
Tall, strong and very hairy
Lucifer is truly scary.

Jacob Roman Lewis (9)
Cyfarthfa Park Primary School, Cyfarthfa Park

My Monster Blobby

Hi, my name is Blobby, I like being snobby
I like to sleep, 'cause that's my favourite hobby.
I like the Spar, 'cause that's my bar
And I like Jupiter, 'cause I get stupider.
That's all for now, 'cause I like brown cows
And I need to get into the bath.

Sophia Gunter (9)
Cyfarthfa Park Primary School, Cyfarthfa Park

Meet Dugs

Hi, I'm Dugs
I like hugs
I like giving big joyful hugs
I like eating slippery slimy slugs
And creepy-crawly bugs
I'm as purple as a potion
I like putting on smelly lotion
I like to spin my propellor round and round
It's like a loading sign on a laptop.

Alys Hocking (8)
Cyfarthfa Park Primary School, Cyfarthfa Park

My Monster Jack

Hi, my name is Jack
I am big, furry, scary,
I am a monster,
And my belly is hairy,

Jack is as tall as a lamppost,
He is bigger than a school,

Hi, my name is Jack,
I am big, furry, scary,
I am a monster,
And my belly is hairy.

Kainan O'Rourke (8)
Cyfarthfa Park Primary School, Cyfarthfa Park

Loveday

Monsters, monsters,
Big and small,
Some are scaly,
Some are tall.
Some scare you with their tails,
Some scare you with their nails,
Some can be slimy,
While one is named Tiny.

Monsters, monsters,
Big and small,
Oh, how I *wish* you weren't here at all!
'Cause when I go to bed at night,
You give me such a terrible fright.
Every time I go to sleep,
I dream and dream and then I weep.

But... monsters, monsters,
Big and small,
Some think they're extra cool.

Monster Poetry - Funky Fiends

But this one monster,
Called Loveday,
Scares you in a different way.
She doesn't even try to scare,
She shows you love, affection and care.

Together we had the *best* adventure!

We went to:
Asia, Africa,
North and South America,
Antarctica, Europe,
Finally Oceania.

We ate loads of food like:
Waffles, pancakes, cereal and toast,
Pizza, salads, pasta and roast.

So, monsters, monsters,
Big and small,
Aren't the worst after all,
Somewhere there, deep in their heart,
They're kind, happy and even smart.

So, when you're scared please don't fear,
Look under the bed and here,
Right there, don't you see?
You're going to be as happy as happy can be,
Because one day,
You may see...
Loveday!

Rio Richardson (10)
Gulval School, Penzance

Count Your Blessings!

I am a gratitude monster,
And I'm as small as monsters go,
But when it comes to finding blessings,
There's something you must know.

My eyes are round and big,
And blessings I can see,
If you'll help me look for blessings too,
Then grateful you will be.

So let us look together,
And count our blessings, you and I,
And if we truly look,
There are blessings we can spy.

Beau Nash (10)
Gulval School, Penzance

My Monster Rooney

My monster is called Rooney,
He has wild, curly hair,
He has one vast, sapphire eye,
His favourite food is a pear.

My monster is as kind as the king,
He has legs like twigs,
His arms are long and thin,
His favourite animal is a pig.

My monster is very adventurous,
He often travels around space,
When he visits other planets,
He is very respectful of the place.

Jonty
Gulval School, Penzance

All About Claws

My monster is very feisty,
My monster is extremely spine-chilling,
My monster has massive snapping jaws,
His growl is very fearful,
His extraordinary hair goes down to his knees,
Enough about Claws, let me talk about his cave.

His cave is dark and gloomy,
It is made out of stone and rubble,
His cave is not the cosiest thing,
But he calls it...
Home!

Amy Nudd (9)
Gulval School, Penzance

Slippery Slurpus

S lurpus is a slippery, vicious creature,
L ikewise to a snake,
U nusual-looking slimy goo covers him head to toe,
R apidly he dashes at his prey,
P owerfully Slurpus gulps down people like pancakes,
U nnaturally this being stands at a whopping eight feet,
S pookily the beast only becomes visible at the crack of dawn.

Riley Marment (10)
Gulval School, Penzance

Sea Monster

Mysterious mist blankets the bay,
Chasing the fishing boats away.
A peculiar shape jumps and jives,
Big and black, it crashes and dives.
Under the wild, wondrous waves it spins and swirls,
Eerily emerging, it spirals and curls.
Tentacles reaching like giants' fingers,
Under the sea, the monster lingers.

Dexter Cudmore (9)
Gulval School, Penzance

Monster Splot

M ischievous monsters roam our land,
O ngoing mysteries lie on the streets,
N ot many people believe they exist,
S plot is an unknown monster,
T errifying shadows surround him,
E arly evenings he sneaks around catching fish,
R oads drift away as the evening floats on.

Freya Mann (10)
Gulval School, Penzance

Hairy Egg

H e is a great fellow.
A ll the monsters aren't that scary.
I n a talent show, he would win.
R unning is his favourite hobby.
Y es, he needs a shave.

E gg-shaped monster.
G osh, he doesn't have arms!
G ood baked cakes he makes.

Oliver Harvey (10)
Gulval School, Penzance

Who's Hiding In Your Closet?

Do you hear disturbing noises in your closet?
Is it making monster sounds?
Just creep up behind it and shout, *"Boo!"*
Did it run?
Did it yelp?
Did it crawl under your bed?
Then shout, *"Go and hide in someone else's closet, Not mine!"*

Liliana Uddin (10)
Gulval School, Penzance

The Monster Under Your Bed

What is the monster under your bed?
It might be hairy with fangs,
Or it might be scary but really nice,
It could be a teddy bear with five eyes,
It doesn't matter what it is,
As long as you say what it is everything is fine,
So... speak out and stay safe.

Mya-Rose Thomas (10)
Gulval School, Penzance

Monsters

Monsters can be hairy, ugly, cute and crazy,
Monsters can be nice, angry, mean and happy.
They can be small, large, any size,
If they're mean stay away, if they're nice say hello.
Monsters, monsters, what are they?
Are they creatures or secretly humans?

Jason Stacha (10)
Gulval School, Penzance

Cheeky Monsters

M ischievous monsters
O h no, oh no, they are up to mischief again!
N aughty monsters
S neaking behind you to make you jump
T aking your things as a joke
E very day having a laugh
R eading a book to make you jump
S neaky, sneaky monsters.

Molly Barnett (8)
Hasland Junior School, Hasland

Monster From The Moon

There was a silly monster from the moon
Who only ate beef with a spoon
He ate it on the beach
He ate it with a peach
Until his tummy had no room.

Georgia Price (7)
Hasland Junior School, Hasland

Once I Saw A Monster

Once I saw a monster,
It was furry and blue.
Then I thought in my head
That I saw him under my bed.
I thought about it and a voice in my head said,
Imagine all these things I could do
With Jimmy if he got out of bed.
We could go ice skating.
We could go down the red slide
In my favourite park!
We could eat ice cream at the beach.
We could meet Mickey Mouse at Disney World.
And most of all I could...
Take him to my swimming lessons!
In fact, we could also go to the circus.
And all of that only if he stopped sleeping
And got out of bed.

Victoria Lupak (8)
Immanuel And St Andrew CE Primary School, London

The Adventures Of Fufbod

One day, a ball made of fluff,
Decided he had had enough,
He wanted to go out, where it was hot and mild,
Out into the outside world, into the wild.

"A hotel!" he cried. "What a wonderful idea,"
So he looked at the map, to see if one was near,
He stepped out of the house, and into the sun,
To go and have some fun.

There he was, in the hotel,
And he hid behind a sofa,
And suddenly a guest came in,
And he sat on his bed,
And Fufbod made some mischief,
He jumped all over the guest,
And made himself into a pillow,
Nothing happened, thought the guest,
And that is the story of Fufbod, the end.

Cecily Chandler (7)
Immanuel And St Andrew CE Primary School, London

The Journey

There once was a creature called Fuzzyball
Who came from outer space.
He lived on Fuzzland
And had a funny face.

One day he flew away
With his friend called Bat.
They soared up high through the sky
Until they realised Bat had lost his hat.

"Oh no, my hat, my very special hat!" shouted Bat,
"I can't fly without it on my head.
It has super-duper powers!"
And down he fell and landed on his bed.

Fuzzyball followed, desperate to save his friend
For mates should always look out for each other
No matter what happens in the end.

Ada Vening (7)
Immanuel And St Andrew CE Primary School, London

Hooray! Here's My Little Monster

Here's my little monster kind and free
Here's my little monster and he says, "Whee!"
Here's my little monster that walks with me
Is my little monster playing hide-and-seek?
Oh there's my little monster sitting by a tree
Oh my little monster, you've been here a week
And here comes my mum bringing some tea
Friendship little monster, friendship is key
Now my little monster, play with me!

This is my little monster, one, two, three
Who is your little monster on your knee?

Noah Gilson Organe (8)
Immanuel And St Andrew CE Primary School, London

Oh, Rascal!

Oh, Rascal! Oh, Rascal!
Your teacher is mad!
Why are you always this bad?

Oh, Rascal! Oh, Rascal!
Do as you're told!
Or else you'll get a very big scold.

Oh, Rascal! Oh, Rascal!
I can't eat my lunch!
Why did you have to give it a munch?

Oh, Rascal! Oh, Rascal!
Stop gnawing the table!
Can't you see you're upsetting Mabel?

Oh, Rascal! Oh, Rascal!
The day's at an end.
You've really driven us all around the bend!

Keya Edmonds (8)
Immanuel And St Andrew CE Primary School, London

Little Curious Monty

Little Monty lived with me
She asked me so many questions
That I couldn't even see
She was so hairy that we couldn't even breathe
She was very naughty but also very haughty
When we were swimming at the beach
She wanted to reach the bottom of the sea
Suddenly my curious little Monty bumped into a rock
And her mouth plumped because she lost a tooth
And she couldn't eat a yellow fish
That was at the bottom of the sea.

Cesia Ester Medina (7)
Immanuel And St Andrew CE Primary School, London

My Monster Friend

Don't be afraid,
I'm under your bed,
I mean no harm...
I want to be your friend!

Don't be afraid,
I come from far away,
I lost my way here,
And came to hide under your bed!

Don't be afraid,
You look scary too.
But I am kind,
And won't say that to you!

Don't be afraid,
I truly mean no harm,
If you give me a chance,
I promise we will have a lot of fun!

Jagoda Lakos (8)
Immanuel And St Andrew CE Primary School, London

Kelly The Mean Monster

Kelly the mean monster, one, two, three
Kelly is the meanest you will ever see
She peers through trees with a big, beady eye
She's as mean as an ogre, I'll tell you why
She is green with spikes all over her thigh
She likes it, I don't know why
She lurks in the forest with a parrot
All red and green and a black nose for sniffing trees
This is the end, one, two, three
Oh, let me see!

Leila-Marie Stewart (8)
Immanuel And St Andrew CE Primary School, London

Monster Poem

The monster goes to his friend.
And he has two friends.
His friends are brothers.
We play very well.
The mother makes food.
The food is good.
She makes tea.
The tea is good.
We feel joy because we see each other.
We go to my house.
She says my house is big.
I say, "Yes, my house is big."
"It was a good day," says the monster.
This poem is from Monster!

Matiya Kouakou (8) & Mariette Kouakou (8)
Immanuel And St Andrew CE Primary School, London

Monster Of Friendship

Do you know the monster with pink fur?
Do you know the monster with big blue eyes and a big smile?
Do you know a monster with heart-shaped wings?
If not, you must know that he exists!
When friends argue, he shows up... and starts sneezing...
Because he is allergic to arguments and sadness.
And no one knows why his sneezing makes friends calm.
And *friendship* can still be joyful!

Maya Barczyk (8)
Immanuel And St Andrew CE Primary School, London

What Was That?

What was that? Was it a rat or a bat?
What was that? Was it a cat or a mat?
What was that? Was it a tree or a degree?
What was that? Was it a monster or nonsense?
Was it Scar Face or Do Your Lace?
What was that? Was it Scar Face or Do Your Lace?
Was it the monster in the yard?
What was that?

Grace Wikeley (8)
Immanuel And St Andrew CE Primary School, London

Kuthulu's Claws

Kuthulu's claws are sharp
They're really sharp indeed
He's prowling in the dark
Running like a ninja
Sneakily he's gonna pinch ya
Kids run away from him
Kuthulu nearly catches prey that's thin
Kuthulu's claws are really sharp
Really sharp indeed.

Jack Leevi Dean (8)
Immanuel And St Andrew CE Primary School, London

Monster Poetry - Funky Fiends

I'm A Scary Monster

He's a monster
A very big monster
He looks cute and small
But when you scare him
He is humongous with sharp teeth
And a big, red body
If you want to calm down the monster
You have to give him a cookie
A fresh new start
And a cuddle for fun and to be kind.

Zuzanna Szmulska (8)
Immanuel And St Andrew CE Primary School, London

The Purple Dragon

If life stops and you concentrate on the last thing,
You'll find something sleeping,
Through the world of cries and weeping,
And if you get through this world you'll see,
A happy place you wouldn't think of,
And in the centre is a purple dragon,
A world that is full of pleasure,
With happy entities that are clever,
And keep their land safe and pray well,
To the only religion they'll ever tell,
To one creation that has seen all,
And never forget for there's always been,
A small purple dragon,
This place is always battered with smoke,
And shaken and torn until there's no more hope,
But this land is still held together,
There are not millions or hundreds of this,
But only one that destroys the abyss,
And that is the purple dragon.

Lily Johnson (9)
John Rankin Junior School, Newbury

Chloe The Cute Monster

Hello, I'm Chloe the cute monster,
Even though I look like a ghost.
But I'm very good.
Sometimes people say, "How could..."
But I never let them finish,
I always run away.
I also try and be nice to myself.
Did you know I'm going to be
Vice president when I grow up?
Because I never really liked
Being the centre of attention.
I find dice really interesting.
How can something have six sides?
Oh, oh, my favourite food is
Rice with beans and curry.
Wanna hear the thing I hate?
I only hate a few things
And they are mice and lice,
Just imagine insects
Growing and laying eggs in your hair.
Ugh!

Anushka Joshi (9)
John Rankin Junior School, Newbury

Monster Zoo

If you want to make a monster zoo
You're going to have some monsters too
Choose your type.

One eye, two eyes or maybe even a hundred eyes
If you can't think of a torso then draw something that's also
Monstrous.

Make a monster zoo
Make a monster zoo
Make a monster zoo
What else can you do?

One leg, two legs or maybe even no legs
Shapeshifter, scary or maybe even hairy.

Make a monster zoo
Make a monster zoo
Make a monster zoo
What else can you do?

Isobel Healy (9)
John Rankin Junior School, Newbury

Fireball

Fireball is a dragon who is venomous and lonely,
He loves to fly around but he can only go slowly,
He lives in a cave that's dark and wet,
And there he lies with Beatle his pet,
He tries to sneak out of his deep, dark cave,
To be able to do that he has to be brave,
If you ever met him you'd find him cheeky,
And in hide-and-seek, he's always sneaky,
So that's the end of Fireball's story,
I hope you didn't find it a bit gory!

Phoebe Avarne (9)
John Rankin Junior School, Newbury

Monster Cat

Pom Pom was a monster cat,
She ate ice cream so she became fat,
At night she slept on a mat.

Pom Pom was a monster cat,
Once she even chased a rat,
She made the rat go splickity splat,
Sometimes she wore a high-top hat.

Pom Pom was a monster cat,
Bye-bye Pom Pom.

Emily Allan (9)
John Rankin Junior School, Newbury

Monster Poetry - Funky Fiends

Oh My Little Slimy Monster

My friends call me Ady
And I am a very little slimy monster,
I come from Tomansion,
Don't be fooled by my size,
I have fangs and a very grizzly smile
And I love scaring off dogs and cats
In the park.

Nilesh Sharma (9)
John Rankin Junior School, Newbury

Mr Fluffs

M illion IQ, so much it can open doors, even if the door is locked.
R uffles in cuteness but is actually really deadly and has a giant mouth as big as you.
F ire in her eyes, horrifying teeth and full of murder.
L oving too, evil little fluffball.
U ltimate villain.
F ull of nightmares and fear.
F luffy until she gets angry.
S he can be your pet only if you want to die.

Emily Budge (9)
Miller Academy Primary School, Thurso

Monster

M y monster is tall with big feet, he loves to eat bananas.
O n Monday my monster eats the cat litter box, yuck!
N o Bob! He keeps smashing plates and eating my blanket.
S uddenly he's being good, he's happy now.
T here he is, sleeping in my bed.
E verything smells of avocados, I have to clean every day so it doesn't smell.
R ude little Bob, he's so tall but short?

Skye Brock (9)
Miller Academy Primary School, Thurso

Monster

M y monster is so monstrous.
O n some days my monster is always going on adventures.
N early every day my monster goes to the shop to get energy juice.
S ome days he goes to monster school and when he gets back he tells me everything about it.
T en times a day my monster goes to the park.
E very time he goes to the park he sees his friends.
R emember he is always so cheeky.

Georgia Donogher (8)
Miller Academy Primary School, Thurso

Yoshi

Y oshi has a big shell and is green and cool
O ff he goes on his quests for Mario
S o he goes to the Mushroom Kingdom to get Peach
H e hides in his shell when scared
"I love mushrooms," he said, "they're so yummy. Eat, eat, eat, love eating mushrooms! *Yoshi!*"

Charlie Valente (9)
Miller Academy Primary School, Thurso

Alien Puppy

A cute little puppy.
L ittle monster.
I nvisible.
E very time I see you I love you.
N o, you will not kill people.

P uppy dog.
U mnumnum, I like pizza.
P lease give me cuddles.
P lease give me more.
Y es, that's the spot.

Maisy Campbell (9)
Miller Academy Primary School, Thurso

Molly

- **M** olly is really into adjectives
- **O** n Fridays she picks up all the rubbish and she kisses me all the time
- **L** ime is her favourite ice cream, she said it's the juiciest flavour
- **L** ovely sunshine shines on Molly
- **"Y** ay!" shouts Molly in excitement.

Lana Simpson (8)
Miller Academy Primary School, Thurso

My Monster Daisy

On a lovely sunny morning,
Daisy brewed herself a pot of coffee,
Had a love tart for breakfast,
Went outside and smelled lovely flowers,
Said hi to the bees
And went off in her pink car.
She said hi to everyone
And had a great day,
Then got in her bed and slept.

Charlie Litchfield (9)
Miller Academy Primary School, Thurso

Monster

M y monster is called Shay.
O h, Shay has a pet octopus.
N ice Lamborghini, Shay.
S hay has gone to school today.
T onight for dinner we are having pizza.
E very day after school I go to the swing park.
R evvy is Shay's dog.

Adam Clark (9)
Miller Academy Primary School, Thurso

Fruity

F ruity is as fluffy as a cloud.
R ed and blue, all the fruit colours.
U nlimited powers and he is so funny.
I think he's fun and super cool.
T he trickster he can be.
Y es, he's funny and super fluffy, he's Fruity.

Fraser Mill (8)
Miller Academy Primary School, Thurso

Silk

S ilk is a darkness monster from the dark lands.
I n the dark he hides, in the light he... suffers.
L iving in darkness is not easy, it's evil, full of rage and war, no fun, ice cream or light.
K illing anyone in sight...

Seth Pollard (9)
Miller Academy Primary School, Thurso

Sweet

S he is soft, kind, sweet and cute
W ill she trick you? She is a devil
E xceptional, impressive, cool
E mma is her best friend
T ickle one, sweet and lovely one.

Darcey Shearer (9)
Miller Academy Primary School, Thurso

Kirby

K eeps King Dedede away
I n the land he rides a star
R ound in the Forgotten Land he goes
B oom goes his hammer
Y um! He eats everything in his way.

Struan Sparling (8)
Miller Academy Primary School, Thurso

Pickle

P ickle is amazing
I t's animals he loves
C ats like him
K ing of the dinos
L oving friends
E legant, loving dino loves everything.

Anya Livingstone (9)
Miller Academy Primary School, Thurso

Mr Worries Is My Monster

First, there's a rhythm, you'll need to clap
Keep that rhythm and stay in time
Because Mr Worries needs to talk
And it needs to rhyme!
"The only thing I want to do
Is take all the worries out of my friend
And keep her happy
But to do that we rhyme to each other like this!"
Mr Worries you are the best
Do you want a worry?
It can be a curry
Now we have to go but first
We need to say thank you for listening
And we will mosey until we go!

Nevaeh King (9)
Revoe Learning Academy, Blackpool

Monsters

Some monsters are big and small.
Some monsters eat pigs on straw.
Some monsters have four legs.
Some monsters have more legs.

Monsters are like you and me.
So when you see a monster call them he or she.
Monsters are all around us.
So you might see one on a bus!

Monsters are beautiful and nice.
Even though they eat mice!

Layth Essaadi (8)
Revoe Learning Academy, Blackpool

Introducing Devil

My monster's name is Devil
And he is a rebel
You see, he's mean and naughty
But he's rather nice and sweet
He doesn't have friends
So you could make him some
He might rather scare people
And live in a cave
But really he's kind and soft
And he is rather delicate.

Cayla Sowerby (8)
Revoe Learning Academy, Blackpool

Giggles

My name is Monster Giggle,
I live in Giggle Land.
I have a best friend called Holly,
We like to eat ice cream and lollies,
Sitting on the sand.
I am a friendly monster,
I dance and play all day.
We love to go to Florida,
Where it's nice and hot.

Holly Sharman (9)
Revoe Learning Academy, Blackpool

Soglin

There was a little goblin,
He was called Soglin,
His friends called him that,
Because he was like a soggy mat,
With a floppy hat,
And that was the end of that.

Xander Wood (9)
Revoe Learning Academy, Blackpool

Octo Demon

Do you know Octo Demon?
He's kind
With a precious mind
And from an island
In Thailand
And he's a good friend
And he always lands.

Ramy Essaadi (8)
Revoe Learning Academy, Blackpool

Blobby The Monster

One day, I was walking in a forest and I saw a monster,
But when I brought him home he wasn't really a bother.
He was very kind and he was as green as a pea,
He liked to build sandcastles and play by the sea.
Blobby liked to eat sandwiches, chocolate and tins,
But sometimes he just liked eating some pins.
The next day, Blobby and I were at the park,
When he suddenly heard a loud dog bark.
Blobby was super scared of big dogs,
But then he said he was also scared of bogs.
The brown, angry dog tried to attack Blobby and he almost got eaten,
So I saved him by pushing the dog into a log and then it was beaten.
Later that day, Blobby and I went to our house,
And our house, which was a cave, was very safe.

Ryan Conlisk (8)
St Mary's RC Primary School, Edinburgh

King Dark

K ing Dark is his name
There is no one to blame
For that horrible name
Great my monster is
Because he is super cool
But misunderstood.

I wonder if he thinks
To himself all the time
About different things.

N ever try and fight my monster
The mightiest monster ever
He is dark and scary
With talons, fangs on his chest
And he also seeks blood.

G ood he is not
He is dark, dark and cruel
He will kill, kill, kill, kill, kill and kill
Until he gets what he wants
My monster may not talk

But he can understand me somehow
Plus he has a third eye
That has an additional power
That makes him ultra-strong.

D ark is the king of the planet Sadly
It is the bounciest, most fun
Biggest and most joyful planet
In the universe.

A tragic accident happened
Twenty-four years ago
It was 1999
The Dark Emperor Goza
Almost took over the entire universe
With Dark Gotengeta the guardian
He blew up the ship to stop them.

R evenge is what he wanted on Gotengeta
It is all he wanted also because
He was the only one stronger than King Dark.

K ing Dark is the killing king
So he finally destroyed Gotengeta
Once and for all
By making him look into his third eye
That blew him up
But Dark got seriously damaged
And died.

Coburn Dalli (8)
St Mary's RC Primary School, Edinburgh

My First Day At School

Last week was my first day at monster school
My dad thought it would be very cool.
I saw lots of monsters, yellow and green
It was the most monsters I'd ever seen.
My first class was science, we learned about space
Plus my teacher gave me a new case
Full of pencils as colourful as a rainbow.
My second class was maths
We learned about division
But I had a big confusion.
Then it was break
I sat with my friend Jake
He was as yellow as the sun.
We went to our trays and got our stuff
Then it was writing class, that was fun
Because I got picked number one.
After that it was home time, I was glad
'Cause I would see my dad.
He was glad to see me too.

Amelie Prestage (8)
St Mary's RC Primary School, Edinburgh

When I Was A Hero

Last week I was walking down a street,
Until I saw some men in front of me,
I could only just see them for they were dressed in black,
I could also just make out a big, bulging sack.

They were trying to break into someone's house,
And they hadn't noticed me for I was as quiet as a mouse,
I looked around, trying to think,
And then it came to me quicker than a blink,
I would ring the other doorbells,
And they would call for help.

I knocked rather rapidly at a door,
A monster came, her appearance looked quite sore,
Comparing her brown skin and wariness,
To my wings and hairiness.

"Yes," she said and my whole story came pouring out,
That was for certain, without a doubt,
And then she stuttered, "Are you sure?"
I said, "Deadly serious and nothing more,"
And that was how I was a hero for a day,
As she called the cops and the men were taken away.

Agnes Johnston (8)
St Mary's RC Primary School, Edinburgh

The Time I Met A Monster

One day, I was walking to the park,
And it was getting quite dark,
I looked on the swings,
And saw a thing,
It came up to me and introduced itself.
Her name was Bonnie,
And she had an interesting hobby,
She also told me she was from Planet X55,
I said goodbye and walked home.
But Bonnie followed me all the way back,
I knew she was lost, so I let her stay the night.
The next morning, she gave me a bit of a fright,
Bonnie said that she needed to go home.
I told her that it was fine to go,
And to go slow when going down the stairs.
I watched her leave outside my window,
While also waving goodbye.
And that was the time I met a monster!

Emma Patterson (9)
Strabane Primary School, Strabane

Monster Poetry - Funky Fiends

Ninja Hammer

In the garage, on a high-up shelf,
Lives the strong and speedy Ninja Hammer,
Alongside him live Ninja Chainsaw,
Strimmer, Drill, and Axe,
He's a ninja orange belt warrior,
He knocks out those bad tool robbers,
His knock-outs look so easy,
He has them on the ground with a crash and a smash,
He's as quick as a dash,
So, folks, if you need your car fixed,
My friend, Ninja Hammer's garage will do it in a tick,
He'll not rob your tools,
Instead, he'll sort your fuel,
He's one-of-a-kind,
He'll help you if you're in a bind,
On my list, he's way up high.

Cameron Foy (9)
Strabane Primary School, Strabane

McDonald's Monstrosity

Hi, my name is Jack,
I was feeling kind of blue,
So I went to McDonald's,
And met someone I knew.

It was my brother, Phoenix,
He got a Happy Meal,
There was a monstrous toy inside,
It really made him squeal!

It was Paul the peanut panda,
He looked cute but he was sneaky,
He sneaked all the way from China,
He was really cheeky.

He was very chubby,
With fangs that open peanuts,
He scared all the customers,
And made my brother go nuts.

I calmed him down with McNuggets,
He turned nice, not angry,
He's not a monster now, we're friends,
Turns out Paul was just hangry!

Farrah Mcgerrigle (9)
Strabane Primary School, Strabane

The Witty Monster

There was a monster called Boyle,
Who lived near the river Foyle,
He liked licking lovely lollipops,
He always tripped and he always flopped,
He entered a competition for the most witty monster,
But first, he went to eat a lobster,
He started to feel sick a lot,
Luckily, he had medicine that he bought,
Then he walked to the building,
He wasn't allowed, but he was willing,
So he went in disguise,
And he got in, which was a surprise,
People thought he was bad, but he was persistent,
People knew his jokes were bum,
Therefore, he won!

Max Thompson (9)
Strabane Primary School, Strabane

Monster Poetry - Funky Fiends

Superhero Sid

Bang! Bang! What's that I hear?
That made my heart jump with fear,
Oh yes, it's Sid!
He's a superhero kid,
He's a cute friendly monster
That lives in my school locker,
He saved me last week,
When he heard me squeak,
Because a bloodthirsty beast
Tried to eat my feast,
Sid gave him a fright,
And he ran away into the night,
The beast is away,
But my friendly monster can stay.

Alex Hamilton (9)
Strabane Primary School, Strabane

The Monster's Day With Me

Hi, I am Crisp, my nickname for me,
I am an only monster, you see,
My love for sweet treats makes me unique,
I walk to the shop to take a peek,
From the corner of my eye,
I see my prize...

A beautiful shiny lollipop!
The server, called Paige, takes my coins,
"Oh, what a delight! That's my favourite too,
Shall we be friends?" she asks,
As we lick on our strawberry and cream delights.

Paige Porter (9)
Strabane Primary School, Strabane

Monster Poetry - Funky Fiends

Miko The Monster

I was flying to a place called Earth,
I arrived and saw a cat,
I also saw a mat,
The cat crawled onto the mat,
I shape-shifted into a dog,
And ran into some fog,
I saw a shop, I crawled over,
I saw a six-leaf clover,
There was an overflow of people,
I left and shape-shifted into a frog,
And hopped onto a log,
I left Earth and went to my planet,
I do like Earth!

Aoibhi Brolly (9)
Strabane Primary School, Strabane

A Metaphorical Monster

There once was a monster who lived under my bed,
Some people have monsters that live in their head,
Mine has green eyes and makes noises when I try to get to sleep,
One night, I decided to have a little peek,
To find a scared little kitten hiding there instead,
So, if you have monsters in your head -
Tell someone and it might turn into a little kitten instead!

Emma Devine (9)
Strabane Primary School, Strabane

Minima Fur

Minima Fur is a tiny monster alright,
He is a thief, he is a thievery chief,
Minima Fur looks for bugs on rugs,
He is a louse in the house,
At night, his sight is bright and filled with blight,
Minima Fur flops and hops in the house,
Causing trouble on the double,
So you better watch out for his tiny snout,
Watch out, watch out, watch out!

Aaron Kingham (9)
Strabane Primary School, Strabane

Monster Poem

My monster's name is Jamal,
He isn't very tall,
He is pretty awesome,
And lives at Cherry Blossom,
His body is really furry,
But watch out, as he is always in a hurry,
He is as strong as an ox,
But sometimes he likes to climb rocks,
We both like to travel to outer space
While singing Amazing Grace.

Blaine Peoples (9)
Strabane Primary School, Strabane

Dot-A-Lot's Wild Adventure!

One day, Dot-A-Lot went to Asda in his Mazda to get some pasta,
Then went to adopt a zebra,
After that, they got Fanta,
Dot-A-Lot made the pasta,
They did a race to see who could eat it fasta!
Last of all, they made popcorn in a pot,
Dot-A-Lot said, "Eat it fast while it's hot!"

Emily McCully (9)
Strabane Primary School, Strabane

Young Writers Information

We hope you have enjoyed reading this book – and that you will continue to in the coming years.

If you're the parent or family member of an enthusiastic poet or story writer, do visit our website **www.youngwriters.co.uk/subscribe** and sign up to receive news, competitions, writing challenges and tips, activities and much, much more! There's lots to keep budding writers motivated!

If you would like to order further copies of this book, or any of our other titles, then please give us a call or order via your online account.

Young Writers
Remus House
Coltsfoot Drive
Peterborough
PE2 9BF
(01733) 890066
info@youngwriters.co.uk

**Join in the conversation!
Tips, news, giveaways and much more!**

 YoungWritersUK 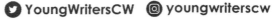 YoungWritersCW  youngwriterscw

Scan me to watch the
Monster Poetry Video